FROM
IDEA
TO
REALITY

AN ENTREPRENEUR'S GUIDE TO
MEANINGFUL BUSINESS GROWTH

JEAN PAUL PAULYNICE, MBA

PAULYNICE CONSULTING GROUP
Your Success Is Our Business!

ISBN: 978-1-7330427-1-0 (Hardback)
ISBN: 978-1-7330427-2-7 (Paperback)
ISBN: 978-1-7330427-7-2 (eBook)

Printed in the United States of America.

CONTENTS

DEDICATED TO EVERYONE
LOOKING TO BUILD A
BUSINESS FUELED BY
PURPOSE AND PASSION.

MAY YOU LIVE WITH
COURAGE, ALWAYS!

Acknowledgment

I want to thank my loving and supportive wife, Bency, and my two beautiful daughters, Saïdah and Elyse, who provide unending inspiration. This book is for you. For all your many talents and the endless love and laughter we share. It's when I'm with you that I am blissful.

I also dedicate this to my grandfather, Andre, who raised and shaped me to become the successful man I am today and whose eternal love and guidance are with me in whatever I pursue. Grandpa Andre, you are my ultimate role model.

CHAPTER ONE

THE ESSENTIALS OF BUILDING A BUSINESS

*This cannot be the year of talking, of wishing, of wanting. **This has to be the year you get it done!***

> \- Eric Thomas,
> Motivational Speaker,
> Author, and Minister

Building a business is one of the most exciting journeys upon which you will ever embark. As a business leader, you will encounter a continual succession of adventures. There will be moments of learning, failing, moving forward, and upward. Even when times are challenging, keep in mind that you will eventually succeed beyond your wildest imagination. *Why*, you ask? How do I know? Because you are fueled by your never-ending, limitless passion and purpose, the secret to success.

Ask any entrepreneur, including myself, the amount of time, effort, and energy that go into all of the different aspects of creating a business, and they will tell you, it is astonishing.

When you think you know everything, you will find there is still more to learn. Don't be concerned. If you are passionate enough and have a clear vision of what your success will look like, you will find the energy and enthusiasm to learn everything you need to know along the way.

With enough passion and purpose, you will be unstoppable, and the essentials of building a business won't overwhelm you.

As a successful entrepreneur, I found that my passion and purpose have served me well. As a prosperous entrepreneur, I know for a fact that *it is the only way you can be*. Passion is what fires you up along the way, and your purpose sustains you through anything.

The only wish I have is that someone would have created this book for me when I was starting. There is so much to learn about building and growing a successful business. You need to understand funding, networking, creating new products, implementing strategy, launching viral marketing campaigns, the ins and outs of public relations, and yes, building branding strategies as well. Moreover, this is just the beginning.

What I'm delivering to you here is a guide to give you clarity, focus, and an amazing action plan for growth. I have drawn from everything I know and also best practices from business leaders around the world. The information has been organized into a convenient workbook to help you operate and market your business successfully.

The only thing you need to bring to the table is your passion, your purpose, and a willingness to learn.

You will learn several things in the workbook. First, some of the best tips, advice, and recommendations I give my clients. Secondly, you will be taught practical ways to structure your business for growth and how to market your products and services daily. Thirdly, you will receive access to my growing community of smart, ambitious, and inspiring entrepreneurs.

Warning! You will get your hands dirty with this workbook. It is made specifically for you, and no two people will use it the same way. It goes deep and wide and will get you thinking about all the different aspects of your business and yourself. It takes you from A-Z in business and includes everything you could imagine and much that you might never have thought about until now. For example, you will learn how to craft the ultimate customer and client promotions, along with how to develop unique incentives to help you launch competitive sales strategies, and exciting and new ways to collaborate with other entrepreneurs. Finally, my favorite topic, how to share your authentic and original story with the world.

There are many business books out there for small and large business owners. Why another one, you may ask? Why is this book special? Well, after working with many entrepreneurs and business leaders, I have noticed an unfortunate bias that holds many people back from succeeding. You see, there are many essential aspects involved with the start of every business, but most entrepreneurs only focus on opening doors and building revenue. They lack the necessary strategy and forget (or don't know how) to be thoughtful about designing a successful brand that will grow into a sustainable company.

Whether you already have a business or you're just beginning to start one, this workbook was developed to help you take it to the next level and *beyond*.

The workbook is written from my professional experience with many ambitious and intelligent people who are based not behind a desk at a university, but in the real world. They are creating exciting businesses just like yours, and they are fired up with passion, just like you. I am not saying that formal education doesn't matter. I, myself, have an MBA. My point is, this workbook will help you fast track your way to success with the essentials you previously might have only learned from an additional four years of schooling.

This workbook is for anyone starting any business, from women and men who are teaching students the peaceful power of yoga and meditation, to those launching new tech startups that are disrupting the way we live, work and play; this book is created for you. It's equal parts motivational and instructional and meant for anyone launching their dream idea.

Whether you are designing dream homes or websites, making beats for Hollywood soundtracks, or just getting your training or life coaching certification, this business advice and process will help you.

You will gain an organizational structure and customized marketing plan for any business. Perhaps you fancy yourself a spiritual healer and want to open a spa, or maybe you have a non-profit helping the underserved become leaders in their field, or you could be empowering women through teaching self-care. It doesn't matter what you are creating, the same business and marketing rules apply.

I have held nothing back because I want you to succeed.

When used correctly, this workbook will help you create momentum, make an impact, and deliver huge value to your audience.

It's all in here, **From Idea to Reality— An Entrepreneur's Guide to Meaningful Business Growth.** This proven strategy is a step-by-step guide that provides everything you need to create a brand that prospers.

So, what are the essentials of building a business? We just went over the first two key ingredients - passion and purpose. What else is there? The essentials include branding, identifying your target markets, learning about industry trends, performing competitive analysis, and a promotional pricing strategy, along with understanding your strengths, weaknesses, obstacles, and threats.

The essentials also include creating a five-star customer or client experience, developing an actionable, integrated marketing plan, sharing your story on appropriate social media platforms, optimizing your cash flow and finances, and understanding how to measure your success.

Yes, there are many moving parts to running a business, but you need not get overwhelmed. Rome was not built in a day. If you have a strong mindset and you plan for tomorrow, if you work smart and not hard, and look for expert guidance while collaborating with intelligent and creative people, you will succeed.

CHAPTER TWO

IT STARTS WITH PASSION AND PURPOSE

You have to have a lot of passion for what you are doing because it is so hard. . . If you don't, any rational person would give it up.

- Steve Jobs,
CEO & Co-Founder of Apple

Leaders are people who make things happen, and people who make things happen are filled with passion and purpose. Passion and purpose are the building blocks of a solid foundation of success. They go hand-in-hand with building a dream business.

Your passion and purpose are crucial to your growth; and without this *fire*, you probably wouldn't have gotten this far. Your purpose is like your road map or your navigation system; your passion is the high-octane fuel you need to be successful.

If you are like most entrepreneurs, you are so excited and can't wait to get started, and your head is spinning with many,

many business and marketing questions. This workbook will help you answer all of your questions and help you identify your audience and learn how to market your products and services to them.

It will act as your business coach, your mentor, and help you answer questions about what to do with advertising, if you need a sales assistant, and how to identify opportunities in the market.

The answers to these questions will point you in the right direction, so you can use your passion and purpose to drive your business to the next level.

Your passion and purpose are critical to your success. These attributes are what will help keep you going as you climb the ladder to the top.

A lot of aspiring entrepreneurs do not have a passion for their businesses. They do not even have a passion for making money. They like the idea of success. This attitude is how companies fail.

When I see people who excel in their career or life, I notice that they have a strong passion for what they do. That passion and their purpose make a world of difference.

We have all been around people who have talent and skills but lack the passion for what they do. They might have a top-notch education and all the right strengths to excel, the knowledge, and the experience as well. Yes, they are also excessively equipped to handle their job, but the one difference is they have no interest, and they are disengaged at work. Their heart is not in it.

Now, a few questions for you, to determine just how

passionate you are and to define your purpose in a clear and definite manner.

I. WHAT DO YOU BELIEVE YOUR PURPOSE IS?

---

2. WHY ARE YOU SO PASSIONATE ABOUT THIS?

_____

_____

_____

_____

_____

_____

_____

_____

_____

_____

_____

_____

_____

_____

3. HOW DO YOU REMIND YOURSELF DAILY
   ABOUT YOUR PASSION AND PURPOSE?

_____

_____

_____

_____

_____

_____

_____

_____

_____

_____

_____

4. HOW WILL YOUR BUSINESS REFLECT THIS
   VISION?

_____

_____

_____

_____

_____

_____

_____

_____

_____

_____

_____

_____

_____

CHAPTER THREE

SELF-AWARENESS: UNDERSTANDING WHAT DRIVES & SUSTAINS YOU

Uncovering your passion and purpose
*will be the **biggest adventure of your life.***

- Jean Paul Paulynice,
Author of "It's Time to Start Living with Passion!"

Yes, it is crucial to be full of passion and purpose, but do you know what is even more important than that? **It is vital for you to know yourself. Self-awareness is critical** because it empowers us to make changes and to build on our areas of strength, as well as identify areas where we would like to make improvements. As Aristotle put it so eloquently, *"Knowing yourself is the beginning of all wisdom."*

Self-awareness is having a clear perception of your personality, including your strengths, weaknesses, thoughts, beliefs, motivation, and emotions. **Self-awareness** allows you to understand other people, how they perceive you, your attitude, and your responses to them at the moment.

Before you begin to consider the tactical questions of starting a business, let's look at some of the bigger ones, some of the most important questions to ask yourself, *about yourself*, like. . .

I. WHO ARE YOU? HOW HAVE YOU CHANGED IN THE PAST FIVE TO TEN YEARS?

_____

_____

_____

_____

_____

_____

_____

_____

_____

_____

2. WHAT ARE YOUR BEST ATTRIBUTES? THE CHARACTERISTICS ABOUT YOURSELF THAT YOU (AND OTHERS) REALLY APPRECIATE?

_____

_____

_____

_____

_____

_____

_____

_____

_____

_____

_____

_____

3. WHAT WEAKNESSES ARE YOU WORKING ON RIGHT NOW? HOW ARE YOU MAKING HEADWAY TO IMPROVE YOUR HABITS, YOUR RELATIONSHIPS AND YOUR LIFE?

_____

_____

_____

_____

_____

_____

_____

_____

_____

_____

_____

_____

4. HOW DID YOU BECOME SO PASSIONATE
   ABOUT YOUR IDEA, AND HOW DID YOU
   DECIDE IT WOULD BENEFIT YOU AND THE
   WORLD?

_____

_____

_____

_____

_____

_____

_____

_____

_____

_____

_____

5. WHAT IS MOTIVATING YOU TO BUILD THIS
   BUSINESS? ASK YOURSELF, WOULD IT
   MATTER IF I DIDN'T BUILD THE BUSINESS?
   WHAT ELSE WOULD I DO?

_____

_____

_____

_____

_____

_____

_____

_____

_____

_____

_____

_____

6. HOW WILL YOU BRING YOUR UNIQUE,
   AUTHENTIC PERSONALITY TO YOUR
   BUSINESS?

_____

_____

_____

_____

_____

_____

_____

_____

_____

_____

_____

7. HOW WILL YOU USE YOUR PASSION AND
   PURPOSE TO IGNITE AND FUEL YOUR
   BUSINESS?

_____

_____

_____

_____

_____

_____

_____

_____

_____

_____

_____

CHAPTER FOUR

BUILDING YOUR DREAM TEAM & BUSINESS

*Ideas are the easy part. It's **the execution of the idea** that becomes the difficult part.*

— Mark Cuban,
American Businessman & Investor

While you might hear some people say that being an entrepreneur is lonely, building a successful business requires you to co-create with others. It also makes building your business easier to execute each day, especially when it comes to selling your products and services. It's not easy to represent yourself. Some new business owners are shy about reaching out to connect with other entrepreneurs. They *want* to pursue partnerships and collaborations with others but have an intense fear of being rejected. We all do.

You don't want to impose on others and, even worse, when you do reach out, nobody may respond. It's during these more challenging times that your passion and purpose will empower you. It will give you the motivation, and the drive you need to keep going because it is so important to be 100% certain that you are going to launch something that you feel will help serve the world with your unique talents, gifts, and energy.

Also, many entrepreneurs think that they have to wear all of the hats in the beginning, and sometimes they do.

The business creator, the entrepreneur, is the product creator, graphic designer, website builder, lifestyle photographer, copy and content writer, and the bookkeeping and accounting manager of their business, all at once, but sometimes they burn out.

Take Lauren, for example. She started her own fashion design business about three years ago. At that time, it was just her and her sample making factory. She launched her first few styles on a platform called Shopify. She enjoyed sketching and working with her factory director, creating samples and then sizes, and then her first runs, which were very small, about 20 units of each style.

Lauren promoted her fashion designs on Instagram and gave them to influencers for free, in exchange for a posting. Her following and customer base grew quickly. She was doing everything, from designing to marketing to bookkeeping to graphic design. It was exhausting. It was when her office became packed with boxes that had to get to the UPS office; she knew it was time to find her first helper. That person would ship out her designs to the customers. Her budget was small, but she knew she could no longer do it alone.

The truth is, even if you are on a budget, you don't have to do it alone. In 2019, there is a multitude of resources to use to find the best talent without committing to paying an employee salary and benefits. Yes, eventually, as your business takes off, you will need to hire a team; but in the beginning, when you are just starting, you can save money by working with writers and marketers on Upwork, website builders on Toptal, business experts on Clarity.fm and Guru.com. There is a growing list of freelancers and consultants waiting and eager to help you grow. There is no need to hire someone on payroll immediately, which can be very costly.

Also, before you begin handing out job responsibilities, it is essential to know your strengths and weaknesses. Some of the critical questions to ask yourself include. . .

I. WHAT ARE YOU BEST AT, WHAT ARE YOUR TALENTS AND GIFTS, AND WHERE DO YOU NEED HELP? GUIDANCE? ASSISTANCE?

_____

_____

_____

_____

_____

_____

_____

_____

2. WHAT ASPECTS OF THE BUSINESS ARE NOT WHAT YOU LIKE TO DO?

_____

_____

_____

_____

_____

_____

_____

_____

_____

_____

_____

_____

_____

3. HOW WILL YOU MAKE SURE THAT THE PEOPLE YOU WORK WITH WILL HELP YOUR BUSINESS STAY FOCUSED ON YOUR PURPOSE AND YOUR STANDARDS?

_____

_____

_____

_____

_____

_____

_____

_____

_____

_____

_____

4. WHEN THE GOING GETS TOUGH, AND YOU
   ARE EXHAUSTED, WHAT WILL YOU DO TO
   REMAIN STRONG, RESILIENT, AND
   PERSISTENT?

_____

_____

_____

_____

_____

_____

_____

_____

_____

_____

_____

_____

5. HOW WILL YOU TAKE CARE OF YOUR BODY, MIND, AND SPIRIT AS THE BUSINESS BECOMES MORE AND MORE DEMANDING?

_____

_____

_____

_____

_____

_____

_____

_____

_____

_____

As you build your team and your business, you will need to understand all of this, so that you work with people who compliment your talents, and you know precisely what to do so you don't risk burnout.

CHAPTER FIVE

Why the World and Your Business Needs a More Passionate You

No alarm clock needed.
My passion wakes me.

– Eric Thomas,
Motivational Speaker,
Author, and Minister

When you start using your gifts and talents, you begin to add value to society and your community, and the world-at-large will reward you for that. Yes, this is correct. People in the world will pay good money for things that enhance their lives and their businesses. That's a brilliant result. However, building a business is not simple or easy, and times will get tough.

During difficult times, passion is needed to fuel your soul and keep you moving in the direction of your dreams. Passion is a wonderful tonic for tough times. It works like magic to keep you and your business alive and vibrant, even when you may be exhausted and struggling.

When I think about people with passion, I think about Tyquan. Ty works for a leading insurance agency. He is in customer service who does a great job because he has a lot of pride. He makes a good salary and pays his bills on time. Now, on the weekend, Ty has a passion project. This passion project is the result of his love for making music. Ty makes beats for the videos you see on YouTube and the series you binge on Netflix. Any chance he can get, he collaborates with others to create amazing sounds.

Now, this gives Ty very little free time. When he is not working at the insurance company, he is making beats and reaching out to others in film and video to collaborate. His endeavors sometimes put him on a plane out to Los Angeles on a Friday night and back in his home of New York by Monday at 6:00 AM.

Bleary and literally "red-eyed," Ty will go back to his insurance customer service job by 9:00 AM on Monday, straight from the airport, because he is fueled by passion.

You see, passion is like an energy lightning rod. It will keep you going even when you think it is not physically possible.

- Passion will power you through the late-night writing and editing.
- Passion will propel you to be bold enough to meet those

31

more influential and powerful.

- Passion will potently energize you to face another moment of rejection.

CHAPTER SIX

YOUR PASSION & PURPOSE WILL KEEP YOU HEALTHIER AND HAPPIER

*It's the ultimate luxury to combine passion and contribution. It's also **a very clear path to happiness**."*

- Sheryl Sandberg,
COO of Facebook &
Founder of Leanin.org

Unfortunately, many people would love to start their own business, but they are stuck in a job that they don't even like, and some are afraid to leave because they have too many financial commitments. This stress can affect their health, their family, and their entire life.

Scientific studies have proven that those who know why they are here and whom they are doing it for—those who genuinely know their purpose and the reason they exist—will live longer, stronger lives filled with more joy and passion.

So, you may already have found your passion and purpose.

If so, congratulations! That is wonderful, and hopefully, you see the health benefits right now. The trick is to find ways to keep your passion alive. Everyone excited about an idea for their business begins with passion, but even passion can fade away during difficult times.

Here are some questions to ask yourself to keep your passion and purpose alive.

I. HOW WILL YOU MAKE SURE THAT YOU REMAIN PASSIONATE ABOUT THE BUSINESS?

_____

_____

_____

_____

_____

_____

_____

_____

2. WHAT ACTIVITIES WILL YOU DO TO MAKE
   SURE YOU HAVE THE ENERGY AND
   ENTHUSIASM TO WORK LONG DAYS AND
   WEEKENDS?

_____

_____

_____

_____

_____

_____

_____

_____

_____

_____

_____

3. HOW WILL YOU CONTINUE TO CULTIVATE
   PASSION, EVEN DURING TIMES OF
   DIFFICULTY AND HARDSHIP?

_____

_____

_____

_____

_____

_____

_____

_____

_____

_____

_____

4. HOW FAR WILL YOU GO IN ORDER TO ACHIEVE YOUR DREAM BUSINESS? IN THE EXAMPLE ABOVE, TY COMPROMISES HIS FREE TIME, WHICH FOR MANY PEOPLE IS TOO MUCH TO COMPROMISE. WHAT ARE YOU WILLING TO COMPROMISE?

_____

_____

_____

_____

_____

_____

_____

_____

_____

_____

_____

CHAPTER SEVEN

WHY YOUR STORY MATTERS

*Don't ever allow yourself to feel trapped by your choices. Take a look at yourself. You are a unique person created for a specific purpose. Your gifts matter. **Your story matters.** Your dreams matter. **You matter.***

- Michael Oher,
American Football Player & Inspiration
for the book and film, The Blind Side

Many entrepreneurs shy away from sharing their true story. They feel like they don't want to make the business about them. If they only understood how refreshing and genuine it is to learn about the beginnings of a business from the customer or client's perspective. The truth is, people will be more excited about their "brand" if it has an authentic connection to something that rings true inside them.

Your personal and professional story *is* what will resonate with others. It is the emotional connector between you and your customers and clients.

Your story can be used as a powerful tool to win over a community of people around the world.

I proved this to be true for me when I launched my first book, *It's Time to Start Living with Passion!* I shared my story about finding my purpose in the book and found that it inspired others to do the same. I included my real struggles and made myself very vulnerable. I had to overcome my shyness. People who read the book find my candidness very helpful, and it helps them open up, and they feel safe doing so after reading my book. You see, while we all have different purposes in life, we all share the universal desire for acceptance.

Now let's look at the questions you must answer to delve into deeper insights about your life, career, and business. Again, knowing one's self is the key to writing your story and ultimately realizing your business dream!

I. WHAT IS YOUR STORY? WHAT HAVE YOU STRUGGLED THROUGH? WHAT HAS BROUGHT YOU TO THE PLACE YOU ARE IN LIFE NOW?

_____

_____

_____

_____

_____

2. WHO AND WHAT INSPIRES YOU?

_____

_____

_____

_____

_____

_____

_____

_____

_____

_____

_____

_____

_____

_____

_____

3. WHAT ARE YOU PASSIONATE ABOUT?

_____

_____

_____

_____

_____

_____

_____

_____

_____

_____

_____

_____

_____

_____

4. HOW DOES YOUR BUSINESS REFLECT YOUR
   PURPOSE?

_____

_____

_____

_____

_____

_____

_____

_____

_____

_____

_____

_____

_____

5. WHAT IS YOUR VISION? WHAT ARE YOUR HOPES, DREAMS, AND ASPIRATIONS FOR YOUR BUSINESS?

_____

_____

_____

_____

_____

_____

_____

_____

_____

_____

_____

_____

6. HOW DID YOU COME UP WITH YOUR
   BUSINESS IDEA?

_____

_____

_____

_____

_____

_____

_____

_____

_____

_____

_____

_____

7. WAS THE BUSINESS IDEA THE SOLUTION TO A PROBLEM THAT YOU HAD PERSONALLY?

_____

_____

_____

_____

_____

_____

_____

_____

_____

_____

_____

_____

_____

8. WHERE ARE YOU AT NOW IN THE PROCESS?
   DO YOU STILL HAVE THIS PROBLEM? IS IT TO
   A LESSER DEGREE?

_____

_____

_____

_____

_____

_____

_____

_____

_____

_____

_____

_____

_____

9. HOW HAS THIS PRODUCT OR SERVICE THAT YOU CREATED CHANGED YOUR LIFE?

_____

_____

_____

_____

_____

_____

_____

_____

_____

_____

_____

_____

_____

CHAPTER EIGHT

DEFINING YOUR BUSINESS MODEL

The key to all life is understanding
how to add value to others.

- Jay Abraham,
American Business Executive,
Author & Speaker

Now, for some of you, you may feel that there is a lot about your business that you don't know or haven't yet developed, as you move from idea to reality. That is true for most entrepreneurs. Everyone is always learning. As an entrepreneur with a growth mindset, part of your responsibility is to look for new ways to generate more value for your customers and new ways to generate revenue for your business. After all, you are ultimately in business to generate sales and make a profit.

The questions that follow will help you think about what you want to achieve as an entrepreneur and help you develop an intelligent business model and plan to accomplish these goals. It will also help you take the time to examine each aspect of your business, to identify weaknesses and opportunities for growth and improvement.

By the end of the section below, you will have developed your answers to questions like – *"What products or services will I offer?" "How will I generate revenue for each one?" "Is there an opportunity to create recurring revenue?"* and *"How will I keep my customers and clients coming back for more?"*

Let's first define what we mean by the business model. A **business model** is a description of how your business intends to operate and make money. Innovative business models go beyond the simple formula of offering a product or service, think of ways to create customer loyalty, provide value in unusual ways, and define new products or services that people didn't even know they needed.

An example of a unique business model would be the disposable razor industry. Think of a company like Gillette. They sell disposable and refillable razors. You pay once for the refillable razor, but you must keep coming back to purchase more razor blades. This promotion is a business model innovation and an important part of their business strategy.

A monthly subscription company, like Birchbox, enables women and men to test new personal care products by paying for a monthly subscription to receive new samples. This subscription is a recurring revenue generator for the Birchbox brand.

Creating a successful business model focuses on the value the business brings to customers and clients, and then develops by growing revenue around that product or service.

Desiree was in public relations for most of her career. After many years, she left the agency she was working at and struck out on her own. That is, she became a freelancer.

She started helping smaller companies with their branding and social media and making a respectable fee for each small business she helped.

Desiree realized that working alone meant she could only help a limited number of people each day. She decided to create her online program for entrepreneurs and charged them to take a video class. This new venture helped her to see that she could "scale" herself and, as a result, make 10, 20 and possibly 100x more than she was making before by helping one person at a time.

a. Establishing a Business Process

Your job as an entrepreneur is to determine your key business activities by first identifying the core aspect of your business's offering.

Key Questions

I. WHAT DO YOU DO/SELL AND WHY WILL PEOPLE PAY YOU FOR IT?

_____

_____

_____

_____

_____

_____

_____

_____

_____

2. HOW DO YOU GET PAID? HOURLY? BY
   PROJECT? ON A RETAINER?

_____

_____

_____

_____

_____

_____

_____

_____

_____

_____

_____

_____

_____

3. ARE YOU RESPONSIBLE FOR PROVIDING A
   SERVICE, SHIPPING A PRODUCT, OR
   OFFERING CONSULTING?

_____

_____

_____

_____

_____

_____

_____

_____

_____

_____

_____

_____

_____

4. WHAT IS THE CORE INCOME GENERATOR OF YOUR BUSINESS?

_____

_____

_____

_____

_____

_____

_____

_____

_____

_____

_____

_____

_____

5. WHAT ARE THE SECONDARY PRODUCTS OR SERVICES THAT YOU OFFER?

_____

_____

_____

_____

_____

_____

_____

_____

_____

_____

_____

_____

6. HOW COULD YOU SCALE YOUR BUSINESS AND MAKE MONEY WHILE YOU SLEEP?

_____

_____

_____

_____

_____

_____

_____

_____

_____

_____

_____

_____

_____

b. Creating a Demand Generation Strategy

Developing a demand generation strategy is like developing a blueprint of the customer's journey, while also documenting their key motivators for taking action and purchasing one of your products or services. A demand strategy is the same as a marketing strategy - it builds brand awareness and interest in your business, generates leads, and is ultimately designed to close sales.

Key Questions

I. HOW WILL CUSTOMERS FIND YOU?

_____

_____

_____

_____

_____

_____

_____

_____

_____

2. MORE IMPORTANTLY, WHAT SHOULD THEY DO ONCE THEY BECOME AWARE OF YOUR BRAND?

_____

_____

_____

_____

_____

_____

_____

_____

_____

_____

_____

_____

3. HOW CAN YOU "MEET" YOUR CUSTOMER
   ALONG THEIR JOURNEY TO FINDING YOU?

_____

_____

_____

_____

_____

_____

_____

_____

_____

_____

_____

_____

4. WHAT CREATIVE IDEAS CAN YOU COME UP WITH TO LURE THEM TO YOU? WHAT PROMOTIONS AND OFFERINGS CAN YOU GIVE THEM TO SIGN UP, SCHEDULE A CALL, OR MEET WITH YOU?

_____

_____

_____

_____

_____

_____

_____

_____

_____

_____

_____

_____

5. HOW CAN YOU TURN A FIRST-TIME
   CUSTOMER INTO A SECOND- AND THIRD-
   TIME CUSTOMER?

_____

_____

_____

_____

_____

_____

_____

_____

_____

_____

_____

_____

6. WHAT CAN YOU DO TO INSPIRE
   CUSTOMERS TO RECOMMEND YOU TO
   THEIR FRIENDS AND FAMILY?

_____

_____

_____

_____

_____

_____

_____

_____

_____

_____

_____

_____

c. Developing a Winning Value Proposition

A value proposition is the special, secret sauce to winning customers and clients over. It's the thing you do differently. It is unique to you. Your unique value proposition is what makes you stand out from the competition. It is what differentiates you from the rest. You will learn more about your UVP by surveying customers and asking yourself the following questions.

Key Questions

I. WHAT IS UNIQUE ABOUT YOUR BUSINESS?

_____

_____

_____

_____

_____

_____

_____

_____

2. HOW WILL YOUR COMPANY STAND OUT AMONG THE COMPETITION?

_____

_____

_____

_____

_____

_____

_____

_____

_____

_____

_____

_____

3. DO YOU PROVIDE AN INNOVATIVE
   SERVICE, A REVOLUTIONARY PRODUCT, OR
   A NEW TWIST ON AN OLD FAVORITE?

_____

_____

_____

_____

_____

_____

_____

_____

_____

_____

_____

4. HOW ARE YOU BETTER THAN THE COMPETITION?

_____

_____

_____

_____

_____

_____

_____

_____

_____

_____

_____

_____

_____

5. HOW WILL YOU CONTINUE ADDING VALUE TO YOUR CUSTOMERS' LIVES?

_____

_____

_____

_____

_____

_____

_____

_____

_____

_____

_____

_____

_____

d. Identifying Target Customers

Your business won't appeal to everyone, and not all of your customers and clients will be alike. They will fall into "categories" of customers and clients.

For you to hone in on them, you have to segment who they are and get to know more about them. You want to know everything you can about your clientele, including the pain points they have, so you can give them what they want.

Think of ways you can narrow your audience down to two or three particular types of customers or buyer personas.

Key Questions

I. WHO ARE THESE CUSTOMERS?

_____

_____

_____

_____

_____

_____

_____

2. WHERE DO THEY LIVE? ARE THEY MARRIED? HOW MUCH MONEY DO THEY MAKE?

_____

_____

_____

_____

_____

_____

_____

_____

_____

_____

_____

_____

3. WHAT CAREER PATH ARE THEY ON?

_____

_____

_____

_____

_____

_____

_____

_____

_____

_____

_____

_____

4. HOW MUCH DISCRETIONARY INCOME DO THEY HAVE?

_____

_____

_____

_____

_____

_____

_____

_____

_____

_____

_____

_____

5. WHAT DO THEY CARE ABOUT?

_____

_____

_____

_____

_____

_____

_____

_____

_____

_____

_____

_____

_____

6. WHAT COMMON CHALLENGES AND PROBLEMS DO THEY HAVE?

_____

_____

_____

_____

_____

_____

_____

_____

_____

_____

_____

_____

_____

7. HOW DO YOU AND YOUR BUSINESS SOLVE THOSE CHALLENGES?

\
\
\
\
\
\
\
\
\
\
\
\
\
\
\

e. Partnering with Important Business Resources

Your resources are everything your business needs in order to make money. Essentially, they are the things you need just to operate and be in business. If you are opening your own cookie company, you will need a place to bake and the ingredients to make those delicious sweets. In most parts of the world, you will need a special food handler's license. Your resources could be you, your partner, your time, your equipment, your studio, your office, your network – basically, anything you need to build your business. There are so many new types of partners for you to choose from. For example, if you are starting a baked goods company, you could opt for a collaborative kitchen lab space as a partner, to keep costs down. You could buy your ingredients with other food startups to get better bulk prices. You could partner with food bloggers and have them review your cookies to build your network.

Key Questions

I. WHAT MUST YOU HAVE IN ORDER TO BUILD YOUR BUSINESS?

_____

_____

_____

_____

1. WHAT MIGHT YOU BE MISSING TO MAKE IT RUN EASIER? MAKE SURE YOU ARE UP-TO-DATE ON TECHNOLOGY AND ALL OF THE RESOURCES AVAILABLE TO YOU HELP TO MAKE YOUR BUSINESS RUN SMOOTHLY.

_____

_____

_____

_____

_____

_____

_____

_____

_____

_____

_____

2. WHAT WILL YOU NEED TO FIND NEW
   CUSTOMERS AND REACH BUSINESS GOALS?

---

3. IS YOUR BUSINESS BUILT ON
   SUSTAINABILITY? WILL IT GIVE BACK TO
   SOCIETY IN ANY WAY?

_____

_____

_____

_____

_____

_____

_____

_____

_____

_____

The idea here is to make a master list of everything your business will need to become successful. Common resource examples may include a proposal, a spreadsheet, equipment, lease or building purchase, staff, a marketing plan and website, capital, warehouses, intellectual property, and customer lists.

f. Networking with Business Partners and Collaborators

You are not going to be able to build a business alone. Yes, you can be a single operator, but you have suppliers, sub-contractors, those that help you run the business. This can be your assistant, an influencer on Instagram, a fabric supplier if you are in fashion, or your lawyer and accountant.

Key Questions

I.   HOW WILL YOU FIND PARTNERS THAT WILL HELP YOU GROW?

_____

_____

_____

_____

_____

_____

_____

_____

2. WHAT IS YOUR SELECTION PROCESS LIKE?

_____

_____

_____

_____

_____

_____

_____

_____

_____

_____

_____

_____

_____

_____

_____

3. DO YOU HAVE SPECIFIC FILTERS WHEN DECIDING WHO YOU WILL DO BUSINESS WITH?

For example, if you are a green, sustainable business, perhaps one of your filters is that all suppliers must have environmentally friendly processes.

_____

_____

_____

_____

_____

_____

_____

_____

_____

_____

_____

4. HOW WILL YOU NURTURE THESE
   RELATIONSHIPS?

_____

_____

_____

_____

_____

_____

_____

_____

_____

_____

_____

_____

5. HOW WILL YOU DEVELOP A WAY IN WHICH THE RELATIONSHIP WILL BENEFIT BOTH OF YOU?

_____

_____

_____

_____

_____

_____

_____

_____

_____

_____

Now you understand more about why you started the business, how you will build the business, and how you will persevere with passion and purpose. Let's dive into other key elements that take a brand from idea to reality.

CHAPTER NINE

GROWING YOUR PURPOSE, PASSION & BUSINESS

Business is about people. It's about passion. It's about bold ideas.

- Tom Peters,
Author of In Search of Excellence,
Lessons from America's Best-Run Companies

Think of some of your favorite brands. Nike? Reebok? Samsung? Apple? These are more than sneaker and smartphone companies; these brands stand for a promise to deliver quality, but they weren't developed overnight or in a vacuum.

a. Branding

A brand mark represents the sum of people's perception of a company's customer service, reputation, advertising, and products/services. Branding helps people remember who you are, why your company is unique, and usually, a tagline explains why they should do business with you. Branding gives your business a leg up on the competition. It can make your business look bigger than it is, which is especially helpful when you are starting.

Key Questions

I. WHAT WILL YOUR BRAND LOOK LIKE?

_____

_____

_____

_____

_____

_____

_____

_____

2. WHAT WILL YOUR STORY LOOK LIKE ON ALL
   OF YOUR PLATFORMS?

_____

_____

_____

_____

_____

_____

_____

_____

_____

_____

_____

_____

_____

3. HOW WILL YOUR BUSINESS IMPROVE THE
   LIVES OF OTHERS?

_____

_____

_____

_____

_____

_____

_____

_____

_____

_____

_____

_____

4. WHAT PROBLEMS ARE YOU SOLVING, EXACTLY?

_____

_____

_____

_____

_____

_____

_____

_____

_____

_____

_____

_____

5. HOW DO YOU PLAN ON BUILDING YOUR
   BUSINESS DIFFERENTLY THAN YOUR
   COMPETITION?

_____

_____

_____

_____

_____

_____

_____

_____

_____

_____

_____

_____

6. DO YOU HAVE YOUR ELEVATOR PITCH, WHICH IS A SMALL EXPLANATION OF YOUR BUSINESS, PREPARED? GENERALLY, YOU SHOULD BE ABLE TO DELIVER YOUR ELEVATOR PITCH IN THREE MINUTES.

_____

_____

_____

_____

_____

_____

_____

_____

_____

_____

7. DO YOU HAVE A SLOGAN THAT IS EASY TO
   REMEMBER?

_____

_____

_____

_____

_____

_____

_____

_____

_____

_____

_____

_____

8. WHAT WILL YOUR LOGO LOOK LIKE?

_____

_____

_____

_____

_____

_____

_____

_____

_____

_____

_____

_____

9. WHAT ARE YOUR BRAND COLORS?

_____

_____

_____

_____

_____

_____

_____

_____

_____

_____

_____

_____

_____

_____

10. IS THE LOOK AND FEEL OF YOUR COMPANY GOING TO POSITION YOU AS A LEADER IN YOUR INDUSTRY?

_____

_____

_____

_____

_____

_____

_____

_____

_____

_____

Will you create a visual brand guide? Hint: You should! Check out _frontify.com_ to help you create all of your brand assets with your growing team.

Consider website hosting like _https://www.bluehost.com_ and platforms like _wordpress.com,_ which enable you to build a simple and elegant website for your brand.

Benefits

- Branding helps build customer and client recognition.
- Having a strong brand identity works to make your company memorable.
- It will give you a competitive edge in the market and enhance your credibility.

Tools, Techniques & More

What will you name your business? Let namelix.com or brandroot.com help you come up with something catchy.

b. Target Demographics, Customer and Client Personas

Many people ask why targeting a specific market is vital for their business. A target market is a set of individuals sharing similar needs or characteristics that your company hopes to service. For example, new moms are a target market. Tennis players might be a specific target market, freelance graphic designers another. You get the idea.

Identifying a target market helps your company develop effective marketing strategies. Different target markets have different needs, so understanding whom they are by developing "personas" about them can help you do things like set the price of your product, decide where you will sell it, develop the best promotional offers, and choose where you will offer the product, i.e., a storefront, or a website, or both.

Key Questions

I. HOW WILL YOU IDENTIFY AND SEGMENT YOUR CUSTOMERS?

_____

_____

_____

_____

_____

2. WHAT TYPE OF RESEARCH AND TEST
   MARKETING WILL YOU DO TO MAKE SURE
   YOUR MESSAGES AND PROMOTIONS APPEAL
   TO THESE CUSTOMERS?

_____

_____

_____

_____

_____

_____

_____

_____

_____

_____

_____

The Benefits of Targeting Your Customers

- Enables you to laser in on your audience.
- Helps you reach specific demographic groups.
- Helps you connect with your core customers.
- Assists you in finding new customers/clients outside your core.
- Eliminates time wasted promoting to the wrong age, gender, or income.
- Turns your marketing campaign into sales.
- Assists you in creating the perfect social media posts and advertisements that will appeal to your clients.
- Allows you to create segmented campaigns to different types of customers; i.e., single moms, retired veterans, fathers with school-age children, or professional millennials.

Tools, Techniques & More

- Obtaining demographics from sources like **datausa.io**, **City-Data**, **Area Vibes, and Neighborhood Scout** will help you target by zip code, income levels, relationship status, and lifestyle choices.
- Survey tools that allow you to connect with potential customers and markets like **SurveyMonkey.com**, **typeform.com,** and **surveysparrow.com** will enable you to capture feedback with customer/client satisfaction surveys; send a quick poll to get everyone's opinion; connect with your target markets from around the world in minutes; and get pre, post, and live attendee feedback at your next event.

- Even an informal poll on **instagram.com** will help you learn more about your existing clients and customers.

c. Industry Trends

Knowing what is new in your industry and what is coming down the pike in terms of "trends" is an essential part of owning a business. If your customers and clients request some of the newer products or procedures, but you're ill-equipped to adapt and meet those needs, you risk looking antiquated and may lose that business to your competitors. Instead, prepare yourself for the future. Set your business up to meet future demands.

Key Questions

I. HOW WILL YOU KEEP YOUR BUSINESS NEW, FRESH, AND EXCITING?

_____

_____

_____

_____

_____

_____

2. WHAT RESOURCES DO YOU HAVE
   AVAILABLE FOR YOU TO STUDY AND LEARN
   FROM?

_____

_____

_____

_____

_____

_____

_____

_____

_____

_____

_____

_____

3. WHAT WILL YOU DO TO MAKE SURE YOU
   ARE ALWAYS AHEAD OF THE CURVE?

_____

_____

_____

_____

_____

_____

_____

_____

_____

_____

_____

_____

4. HOW WILL YOU AND YOUR BUSINESS CONTINUE TO EVOLVE?

_____

_____

_____

_____

_____

_____

_____

_____

_____

_____

_____

_____

Benefits of Researching Industry Trends

- Prepares you for disruption, especially because technology changes constantly.
- Helps you capitalize on new trends to grow your business.
- Facilitates the understanding of trends to assist with long-term business planning.
- Keeps customers coming back for more new and exciting products and services.

Tools, Techniques & More

- Do your research yearly. Follow your industry's annual trend reports.
- Travel to major cities to research the competition.
- Go to trade shows, seminars, and retreats.
- Subscribe to industry websites.
- Keep an eye out for new technology.

For example, a Yoga studio may look to **wellnessliving.com** for annual trends, a nail salon may visit the **CosmoProfNorthamerica.com** trade show in Las Vegas in July, a dental practice may research **dentistryiq.com,** and a fashion boutique might attend fashion trade shows like the **Coterie**.

Additionally, there are trends for consumer products at **trendhunting.com**, **trendhunter.com,** **WGSN.com** and, of course, **Google Trends**, which will help you find the hottest new search engine queries and products and services to offer.

d. Competitive Analysis

All businesses today are operating in a very competitive and fast-paced environment. Companies are always looking for opportunities to hop on and gain a competitive advantage in the industry. On the other hand, some business owners think that it is best to get on with their plans and completely ignore the competition, while some become so obsessed with tracking their competitors that they even use illegal methods to get the information.

It's best to be the business leader that has strong knowledge about your competitors' strengths, weaknesses, and their activities. This knowledge will help you make better decisions about your marketing strategies. You can't grow a business in a bubble, so keep your eye on the competition.

Key Questions

I. HOW WILL YOU LEARN ABOUT THE COMPETITIVE CHOICES OPEN TO YOUR CUSTOMERS AND CLIENTS?

_____

_____

_____

_____

2. WHAT COMPETITORS WILL YOU HAVE ONLINE? WHAT BRICK AND MORTAR COMPETITORS WILL YOU HAVE?

_____

_____

_____

_____

_____

_____

_____

_____

_____

_____

_____

3. HOW WILL YOU KNOW WHERE YOU ARE WINNING AND WHERE YOU CAN IMPROVE?

_____

_____

_____

_____

_____

_____

_____

_____

_____

_____

_____

_____

_____

Benefits of Performing a Competitive Analysis

- Teaches you everything you need to know about the competition, and then do it better.
- Allows the competition to inspire you.
- Prevents you from marketing in a bubble.
- Enables you to build customer and client loyalty.

Tools, Techniques & More

- Informally survey your customers to find out where they have shopped before.
- Use Internet Tools like **Similar Web** and **Buzzsumo**, as well as AI-powered research like **Alpha Sense** and Wysdom to review your competition and their digital assets.
- Shop and study all aspects of your competition.
- Compete on the details: opening hours, added value, perks & promotions.
- Search and read reviews on **yelp.com**, Google, My Business, and Trip Advisor.
- Let the competition make you stronger.

e. Competitive Promotions

If you are going to grow your business competitively, it is vital for you to know about the positioning, pricing, strengths, and weaknesses of your competitors.

You should know about your competitors' pricing for many reasons. The first is so that you can keep your pricing in line with what people in your target market are willing to pay. Also, you might learn about new pricing models that are more appealing to customers.

It's not always about matching or beating your competitor's price. The point is to understand where your pricing lies in relation to your competitors in the greater market. If your pricing is lower than theirs, this is an advantage. However, you will need to convince prospective buyers that the value of your product or service is as good as those with higher prices.

Key Questions

I. HOW WILL YOU DECIDE TO SET YOUR PRICE POINTS?

_____

_____

_____

_____

_____

2. HOW WILL YOU COMPETE IF YOUR PRICING IS TOO LOW OR TOO HIGH? WHAT MESSAGING WILL YOU USE TO EXPLAIN THIS TO YOUR CUSTOMERS?

_____

_____

_____

_____

_____

_____

_____

_____

_____

_____

_____

_____

_____

_____

3. WHAT CREATIVE PRICING AND
   PROMOTIONAL STRATEGIES WILL YOU USE
   TO ONBOARD NEW CUSTOMERS AND
   CLIENTS?

_____

_____

_____

_____

_____

_____

_____

_____

_____

_____

_____

_____

4. WHAT PRICING WILL YOU USE TO KEEP
   CUSTOMERS LOYAL? TO INSPIRE YOUR
   CUSTOMERS TO TRY NEW PRODUCTS? TO
   REFER THEIR FRIENDS AND FAMILY?

Benefits of Creating A Competitive Pricing Strategy

- Fuels you to go beyond Groupon and train your customers to pay full price.
- Helps you create winning marketing campaigns that build your business.
- Connects you to more loyal customers & clients.
- Helps you create more referrals.

Tools, Techniques & More

- Create seasonal promotions that play on your customer's desire for discounts.
- Emphasize best price points value to build trust, which leads to brand growth.
- Design a strategy to introduce your brand with free offers and complimentary services.
- Create two-for sales and promotions that drive more customers into your business.
- Build bundles of products or services for repeat business.
- Try offering a gift with purchase for the first time and loyal customers.

f. SWOT Analysis

While it sounds more technical than it is, a SWOT analysis will provide the tools and information necessary to establish goals and objectives for your business.

The **S** in **SWOT** stands for **strengths**. These are all how your company, your products, and your services lead the market. You are winning because of your strengths. For example, one of your strengths might be that you are financially unburdened because you have an investor with deep pockets, so you can hire the best people to help you grow right out of the gate.

Another example of strength would be that you have a patent on your product so that nobody can copy your idea.

The **W** in **SWOT** stands for **weaknesses**. An example of weakness could be that you are bootstrapping and you do not have the capital to buy all of the equipment you need to compete.

Another weakness might be that you don't have enough capital to get an impressive office, so you have to meet customers and clients in restaurants and coffee shops.

Another example of weakness could be that you have registered your trademarks, and you have discovered "me too" businesses copying your successful business model. In the world of digital business, where everyone has access to your assets, companies must continually protect their intellectual property and brand marks with tools powered by artificial intelligence like redpoints.com and Welcome.AI.

Perhaps you are a timid person, but your business requires that you network. This inability to meet new potential customers could also be a weakness.

The strengths and weaknesses of business are considered **internal factors**.

The opportunities and threats are considered **external factors**.

The **O** in **SWOT** stands for **opportunities**. You must study industry trends, perform a competitive analysis, and study their pricing and promotional strategies. You want to look for chances to win new customers over with new products, services, and pricing.

The **T** in **SWOT** stands for **threats**. For example, one of your biggest threats could be your own belief in yourself. *Do you feel you are worthy enough to run your own business?* Another example is technology, which seems to be disrupting every industry known to man from banking to health.

When you are performing a SWOT analysis of your business and your competitors, you are not only looking at things like pricing, promotion, and marketing. It would be best if you did a SWOT analysis on all aspects of your business, including:

- Financial Resources – What are your funding, income, and investment opportunities? What are your physical resources? It would be best if you covered everything from your location to the equipment you own.
- Human Resources – Identify the talented professionals you need on your team.
- Natural Resources -- What intellectual property, patents, trademarks, and copyright needs do you have?
- Existing Infrastructure – Have you created an operation manual?

Why would you perform a SWOT analysis on the operations of your business? You may find a way to strengthen your operations manual so that you can build clearer communication tools, so your team can work together more cohesively. You might discover that you need international trademarks. You might learn that your training manual is missing some key training elements to help eliminate errors from your sales team.

Are you courageous enough to examine your business's strengths, weaknesses, opportunities, and threats?

Sometimes it is difficult, to be honest about what you need to focus on to improve. Create a SWOT chart with the tools below to analyze all aspects of your business, and then create a plan to improve.

Key Questions

I. WHAT ARE YOUR BUSINESS'S STRENGTHS?

_____

_____

_____

_____

_____

_____

2. WHAT ARE YOUR BUSINESS'S WEAKNESSES?

_____

_____

_____

_____

_____

_____

_____

_____

_____

_____

_____

_____

_____

3. WHAT ARE SOME OPPORTUNITIES HEADING
   YOUR WAY?

_____

_____

_____

_____

_____

_____

_____

_____

_____

_____

_____

4. WHAT ARE THE POTENTIAL THREATS?

_____

_____

_____

_____

_____

_____

_____

_____

_____

_____

_____

_____

_____

_____

_____

David was working in a co-working space and had a great idea to open up a healthy snack cafe inside their offices. He saw everyone working long hours, drinking soda, and eating chips while sitting at their desks for 15 hours a day.

David had an idea to create an organic cafe for his co-workers, which would offer green juice and salad menu, along with healthier snacks like nuts and fruits. He also had enough savings to buy and prepare some foods and set up the lounge area to look like a cafe.

Members of the co-working space loved it. He would sell out of all of his food by 1:00 PM.

Now, the owners of the co-working space, seeing that David was making money in their location, approached him about "automating" David's healthy snack service.

David went home and decided to make sure he did a SWOT analysis on his healthy business startup.

His Strengths - He created a healthy food menu that people loved and purchased. His salads were handmade, and the co-workers loved his creative, low-fat dressings.

His Weaknesses - For starters, David didn't own the co-working space, so at any time, the owners could ask him to stop selling food to the members.

Opportunities - The members of the co-working space loved his menu, and he could expand it, maybe even to other offices.

Threats - What did the owners of the co-working space mean by "automate"? Did they want to take over the business? Did they think that robots would make salads?

Benefits of A SWOT Analysis

- Remain humble and know thy business while always improving.
- The obstacle is the way - learning how to turn your trials into triumphs.
- Foresee and know pitfalls before they happen.
- Take advantage of new opportunities at the perfect time.
- Understand why you're #1 and learning how to stay there.

Tools, Techniques & More

A SWOT analysis can be accomplished with pen and paper – you can create a list for each strength, weakness, opportunity, and threat you can think of, however; there are more formal tools, like airtable.com, Creately, and smartsheet.com, which help you collaborate with other team members. Your analysis is then easily stored in the cloud and on their platform. These tools help you gather the needed information and organize it in a shareable way for brainstorming sessions and ideation meetings.

g. Creating the Five-Star Customer & Client Experience

Customers and clients will read reviews of your business before they decide to do business with you. Your reviews must be stellar.

The customer experience lifecycle is changing; in today's market, you need to be inventive and transformative to attract, delight, and maintain customers. A five-star rating experience on websites like Yelp, TripAdvisor, and Google My Business starts before your customer has ever touched your product or service and lives far beyond the review, requiring a company culture driven by a uniquely tailored, end-to-end, customer experience lifecycle.

Key Questions

I. HOW WILL YOU KEEP YOUR CUSTOMERS COMING BACK FOR MORE?

_____

_____

_____

_____

2. HOW WILL YOU CREATE THE ULTIMATE
   FIVE-STAR CUSTOMER EXPERIENCE THAT
   LEADS TO WORD-OF-MOUTH MARKETING,
   LOWERING YOUR CUSTOMER ACQUISITION
   COST?

_____

_____

_____

_____

_____

_____

_____

_____

_____

_____

3. WHAT WILL YOU DO IF NEGATIVE REVIEWS COME IN?

_____

_____

_____

_____

_____

_____

_____

_____

_____

_____

_____

_____

4. HOW WILL YOU MANAGE BUSINESS REQUEST CHANGES FROM CUSTOMERS?

_____

_____

_____

_____

_____

_____

_____

_____

_____

_____

_____

_____

_____

Benefits of Creating a Five Star Customer Experience

- Assists you in discovering your community in real life and online.
- Builds your brand loyalty.
- Gives you a competitive edge.
- Communicating builds rapport, trust, and customer longevity.

Tools, Techniques & More

- Take advantage of tools like ZenDesk and FreshDesk.com to help you automate customer service and get feedback from customers with brief online surveys.
- Chat tools like LiveChat.com will make sure you never frustrate a customer again. Once thought of as impersonal, chatbots driven by AI are getting so good, they are having conversations with customers. Check out Twyla.ai
- Responding to customer questions on Yelp and Google My Business will keep you engaged with customers and show you care enough about them to keep them coming back for more.

h. The Importance of an Integrated Marketing Plan

Marketing your business isn't just about Facebook Ads and reaching out to Instagram Influencers. It would help if you thought about where your customers are and how you are going to reach them. It would be best if you were thinking out of the box about your customer's lifestyle choices. Where are they? What do they do outside of work? What time is the best time to reach them? You have to look at all the ways you can reach your customer without stalking them.

Customers don't live on their phones, so look at other ways to connect with them.

- **Print Marketing** because even in this digital age, print is an essential component of an integrated marketing campaign, including flyers, worksheets, handouts, postcards, magazines, newspapers, and posters.
- **Online Advertising** includes banner ads, sponsored content, and Google ads.
- **Email Marketing campaigns** are directed to their inbox.
- **Organic and paid campaigns on social media**, includes Facebook, Instagram, Twitter, LinkedIn, and Pinterest.
- **Writing articles and posting videos** using the power of organic search engine marketing.
- **Outdoor advertising** is useful in billboards and taxi/bus stop advertising.
- **Direct mail marketing** creates promotional offers.
- **Sampling products** delivering monthly subscription boxes.

- **Utilize Pop-up store experiences and meetups** in areas of dominant influence like major cities.
- **Generate social and community events around your local area, city, or state**
- **Create connections and partnerships with other business owners.**

Marketing is about experimentation. The only way to learn how to reach your customers is to try new promotional campaigns. Some will work (do more of those), and some will be less promising.

Presuming you have targeted your customers and created their "personas," for example, what do you know about where your customers go after work? Where do they spend their time online? Learn more about their lifestyle and create integrated campaigns around them.

Key Questions

I. DO THEY HAVE A GYM MEMBERSHIP? IF SO, WHERE IS THE GYM? DO THEY OFFER ON-SCREEN ADVERTISING?

_____

_____

_____

_____

2. ARE THEY HEALTH FOOD STORE CUSTOMERS? IS THERE AN OPPORTUNITY TO SAMPLE TO THEM?

_____

_____

_____

_____

_____

_____

_____

_____

_____

_____

_____

3. WHAT STORES DO THEY SHOP AT AND
   WHAT DO THEY BUY?

_____

_____

_____

_____

_____

_____

_____

_____

_____

_____

_____

_____

_____

4. DO THEY TRAVEL OFTEN? IF SO WHERE?

_____

_____

_____

_____

_____

_____

_____

_____

_____

_____

_____

_____

_____

5. WHAT INFLUENCERS DO THEY FOLLOW?

_____

_____

_____

_____

_____

_____

_____

_____

_____

_____

_____

_____

_____

6. WHAT WEBSITES DO THEY VISIT?

_____

_____

_____

_____

_____

_____

_____

_____

_____

_____

_____

_____

_____

_____

_____

_____

7. WHAT DO THEY DO FOR A LIVING?

_____

_____

_____

_____

_____

_____

_____

_____

_____

_____

_____

_____

_____

8. HOW OFTEN ARE THEY ON THEIR PHONE? WHAT ARE THEIR FAVORITE APPS? WEBSITES?

_____

_____

_____

_____

_____

_____

_____

_____

_____

_____

_____

_____

9. DO THEY HAVE FAVORITE STORES THAT THEY LIKE TO SHOP?

_____

_____

_____

_____

_____

_____

_____

_____

_____

_____

_____

_____

10. WHAT ARE SOME OF THEIR FAVORITE BLOGS? CITIES?

_____

_____

_____

_____

_____

_____

_____

_____

_____

_____

_____

The more you know about your customers' lifestyle, the better equipped you will be at meeting them where you can reach them with marketing messages and product offers. Uniquely targeted campaigns will stretch your advertising dollars, so you can maximize this investment in your business.

Benefits of An Integrated Marketing Plan

- A combination of print, in-store, digital, and social media will reach the customer wherever they are along the journey to finding you.

Tools, Techniques & More

- Using online tools like Hubspot and Hootsuite may make for social media success on Facebook, Twitter, Instagram, Pinterest, and LinkedIn.
- Gathering customer emails for a regular email newsletter using Mailchimp.com.
- Creating a sales funnel to lure customers and clients in with hubspot.com.
- Always networking and bringing in new members using meetup.com and eventbrite.com.

i. Cash Flow & Finances

Staying in the black or "flush with cash" is one of the keys to business success. More than anything else in their businesses, smart small-business owners stay on top of their cash flow, monitoring their balance sheets and cash flow statements monthly to keep their eye on the pulse and heart of their business. These critical numbers tell you exactly how much is coming in and how much is going out of your business. Making more than you're spending? It's all good. Is cash flow regularly edging into the red? Not so good.

Key Questions

I. DO YOU HAVE ENOUGH FOR STARTUP COSTS, THAT IS, TO PURCHASE ALL OF THE EQUIPMENT YOU NEED AND THREE-MONTH'S WORTH OF CASH RESERVES?

_____

_____

_____

_____

_____

_____

2. HOW MUCH ARE YOUR STARTUP COSTS?

_____

_____

_____

_____

_____

_____

_____

_____

_____

_____

_____

_____

_____

_____

3. HAVE YOU CREATED A MARKETING
   BUDGET?

_____

_____

_____

_____

_____

_____

_____

_____

_____

_____

_____

_____

4. WILL YOU BOOTSTRAP OR BORROW MONEY?

_____

_____

_____

_____

_____

_____

_____

_____

_____

_____

_____

_____

5. DO YOU HAVE A LINE OF CREDIT?

_____

_____

_____

_____

_____

_____

_____

_____

_____

_____

_____

_____

_____

_____

Benefits of Focusing on Cash Flow and Finances

- Spend your time building a successful company, not one that is struggling.
- Reduce your reliance on external resources.
- Expand your business and avoid high interest on loans.

Tools, Techniques & More

- Additional sources of funding from PayPal.com & Shopify.com
- Define a one-year, five-year and ten-year plan

j. Measuring Your Success

It's not just operating and marketing your business that matters, it's also measuring your success so you can pivot as you grow.

With the right tools, you will be able to measure what matters and make tweaks to your business along the way.

Of course, you want to measure things like employee productivity and sales revenue. You also want to keep an eye on your gross margin (the profit you make after you deduct your cost of goods sold) and profit margin (the profit you will make after you subtract all of the expenses you incur while doing business).

Some of the most critical aspects of your business to measure include:

Cost of Customer Acquisition

How much does it cost your business to acquire a new customer? Knowing your overhead helps you to understand how much you are spending on your marketing to acquire each new customer. Ideally, you are striving for a zero-customer acquisition cost with word-of-mouth referral. The goal doesn't happen in the beginning, as you are spending money on ads and sponsored content with influencers, but ultimately, if you have created a fantastic product or service, your customers will become brand ambassadors and want to tell their friends and family about you.

Customer Retention

This number measures how long you can keep a customer before they go over to a competitor. The idea is that you want to keep the customer churn rate low. Keeping your customers and clients satisfied will make you more profitable, and that is precisely why you are in business.

Lifetime Value of a Customer

Once you understand how much you can generally profit from a customer after their first sale and throughout their lifetime, you can estimate how much you will need to spend to offer them new products, promotions, and services.

Key Questions

1. HOW WILL YOU MEASURE YOUR SALES GROWTH? YOUR GROSS MARGIN? YOUR PROFIT MARGIN?

_____

_____

_____

_____

_____

_____

_____

_____

_____

_____

_____

2. WHAT REPORTS WILL YOU USE?

_____

_____

_____

_____

_____

_____

_____

_____

_____

_____

_____

_____

_____

_____

3. HOW WILL YOU KNOW IF YOUR MARKETING IS WORKING TO BRING IN NEW CUSTOMERS?

_____

_____

_____

_____

_____

_____

_____

_____

_____

_____

_____

_____

_____

4. HOW MUCH IS IT CURRENTLY COSTING YOU FOR EACH NEW CUSTOMER?

_____

_____

_____

_____

_____

_____

_____

_____

_____

_____

_____

_____

_____

5. WHAT IS THE LIFETIME VALUE OF YOUR CUSTOMER? FOR EXAMPLE, IF YOU SELL SNEAKERS, HOW OFTEN WILL YOUR CUSTOMERS COME BACK TO BUY A PAIR? EVERY SIX MONTHS? WILL THEY BUY YOUR BRAND FOR THEIR FAMILY MEMBERS? ARE THEY NEW PARENTS? IF SO, DO YOU SELL CHILDREN'S SNEAKERS? ETC. DO YOU HAVE A LOYALTY PROGRAM? HOW WILL YOU ENTICE THEM TO SHOP SEASON-AFTER-SEASON? YEAR-AFTER-YEAR?

_____

_____

_____

_____

_____

_____

_____

_____

_____

6. Are you promoting word-of-mouth referral, if so, how? How many new customers are you currently getting from word-of-mouth? How many five-star reviews have you received? Are they leading to referrals?

_____

_____

_____

_____

_____

_____

_____

_____

_____

_____

Benefits of Measuring Your Success

- Measuring your growth will help you increase sales.
- Decreasing your overhead and production costs will help keep things in check.
- Aim to reduce debt and decrease staff turnover.
- Improve the return on your marketing investment.
- Increase digital traffic to your social media pages and website.
- Understand your customer acquisition costs and lifetime value.
- Gain market share, increase repeat business, decrease returns.

Tools, Techniques & Questions for You

- Tools like Salesforce.com will help you measure customer leads, customer loyalty, and your email marketing success.
- SimpleKPI is ideal for small businesses that don't want to pay for a robust dashboard to measure their business.
- When utilized to its fullest, Asana is a great tool to track your team's success, to make sure everyone is meeting goals.
- Also, of course, there is always the old-school spreadsheet on Google Drive.

There you have it! The A to Z essentials of starting a thriving business. Yes, there is much to think about, but as I said from the beginning, it will be your passion that pushes you through. Knowing your purpose will help you face the most challenging parts of learning how to build your brand. *Do you know what else is helpful, especially when you are stuck and need a thought partner?* A group of entrepreneurs to connect with, of course!

CHAPTER TEN

JOIN OUR NETWORK
OF ENTREPRENEURS

*Coming together is a beginning. Keeping together
is progress. Working together is success.*

- Henry Ford,
American Captain of Industry &
Founder of Ford Motor Company

You may be asking yourself, *"Now that I have a better idea of
what is involved in taking my business from an idea to reality, what's
next?*

What else do I have to learn?"

Perhaps you still have some questions about building out
your plan.

We have a growing community of bright business owners
from all walks of life, so be sure to join our **email newsletter** so
you can get updates on workshops, seminars, book launches,
online courses, and more.

Need one-on-one or group consultancy? Our team of
experts is available to help you.

Email your questions to info@jeanpaulynice.com.

We also invite you to join our community of passionate entrepreneurs on **Facebook** at
https://www.facebook.com/jeanpaulpaulynice/

Follow us on **Instagram**
https://www.instagram.com/jeanpaulpaulynice/

Feel free to **Tweet** us at https://twitter.com/paulynice

Connect with us on **LinkedIn**
https://www.linkedin.com/in/jnplnce/

If you are looking for inspiration on how to discover your passion and purpose, check out ***It's Time to Start Living With Passion!***

Are you interested in learning more about how to build your business with social media? Be sure to read Jean Paul's book ***Become a Leader in Your Industry Using Social Media.***

CPSIA information can be obtained
at www.ICGtesting.com
Printed in the USA
BVHW010812090819
555501BV00003B/3/P